Your Way to
Muchness

Teri Leigh

Disclaimer
This publication contains the ideas and opinions of the author and is intended to provide helpful and informative material based on the author's personal experience and knowledge. It is sold with the understanding that the author is not engaged in providing medical, health, or other professional services. Readers should consult professional medical, health and other professionals before participating in any of the practices suggested in this book. The author disclaims all responsibility for liability, loss or risk that is incurred by readers' use and application of any of the contents of this book.

MOZI LLC
www.moziexperience.com
mozi.teri@gmail.com

Book Layout ©2013 BookDesignTemplates.com
MOZI Your Way to Muchness: Body/Mind/Spirit Exercises for Life
Teri Leigh. —1st ed.
ISBN 978-0-9859643-4-4

Contents

To be yourself in a world that is constantly trying to make you something else is the greatest accomplishment.

—RALPH WALDO EMERSON

FORWARD

"Look deep into nature, then you will understand everything better."
~Albert Einstein

Nature never loses its *muchness*. A tree is always a tree, tall and rooted. A bird always sings its perfect song. Animals don't pretend to be something they aren't, unless you've trained your dog to play dead for a treat. So, one of my favorite things to do is go out into nature and meditate to the sounds of birds and wind blowing through the trees as a reminder of what it means to be authentic, natural and true.

One day, I found a majestic oak in an off-leash wooded dog park and sat with my back up against the tree and my legs out long. I hadn't been there more than ten minutes when a family strolled by with three dogs. Their rather bouncy and happy Great Dane (this dog was HUGE) bounded right up to me and sat down next to me. He put his extra large nose right up to my cheek. I squeezed my eyes shut in preparation for a slobbery tongue, but he just gently touched my cheekbone with his soft black nose. Then in one bounce, he leapt over my legs and sat down on my other side. He repeated his gesture on my other cheek. When his family whistled, he bounced away, only to return within a couple seconds to jump over my legs several times. They whistled again, and he bounced away, only to return a third time! The extra-large dog leapt over me several times, bringing smiles and giggles out from places inside me that I didn't know I had. He was honest, authentic, joyful, and fully present in life. He hopped and leaped and bounded through the woods with full zest for life. In just a few moments, he showed me what *muchness* looks and feels like. When his family rounded a bend several yards up the path they called him, "Mozi, come!"

It occurred to me that his name, Mozi, was a shortened acronym for "More Zest" (Mo' Zee), and I knew that this Great Dane and his passion for life was a sort of mascot for my work. The word "mosey" means to wander freely, enjoying the journey without concern for the destination. Mozi the Great Dane was enjoying the journey of his life with great zest, living fully in the moment, unabashedly expressing his boisterous and playful authenticity to everyone he met.

My hope is that this book and the system of exercises provided within it can help you remember you own *muchness* and experience moments of moseying through your own life with zest and authenticity as Mozi did that day under the great oak tree. I invite you to mosey your way through this book, enjoying the process of the journey without focus on any destination, living fully in the moments of remembering your MUCHNESS.

The MOZI EXPERIENCE is a systematic Body-Mind-Spirit educational program designed to teach a simple and applicable practice for remembering your muchness.

CHAPTER ONE

Remember Your Muchness

"You used to be much more 'muchier.' You've lost your muchness."
~The Mad Hatter in Tim Burton's film <u>Alice in Wonderland</u>

Everything, absolutely every single thing about you is perfect. The decisions you make, the body you wear, the mis-steps you take, the beauty you shine, the scars you bear, the successes you live, the wounds you endure, the good deeds you offer, the messes you create, and the character you express are all PERFECT. However, in this ever-changing and chaotic world, it is easy to forget the precious gem that is inside you. People, circumstances, challenges, limitations, and frustrations are constantly trying to make you be something that you aren't. Sadly, in this world, it's so easy to lose your *muchness*.

Muchness - one's most natural state of brilliance, radiance, beauty, strength, confidence and authentic greatness.

I Dreamed a Dream

On April 11, 2009, Susan Boyle, a frumpy woman from a small cluster of villages in Scotland, found her *muchness* on the stage of the popular talent show *Britain's Got Talent* and shared it with the world in a very big way. With a cheeky attitude, the 47-year-old woman shook her hips at the judges and proclaimed she wanted to be as big a singer as Elaine Paige. Judge Simon Cowell flashed his trademark eye-roll prematurely because before she had finished the opening phrase of *I Dreamed a Dream* from the classic musical *Les Misérables,* Boyle received a standing ovation. Upon completion of her performance she started to strut offstage before even hearing the judges' feedback. After being coaxed back to center stage, Boyle heard Judge Amanda Holden confess that she thought the entire audience was against Boyle, but that listening was a complete privilege. Judge Piers Morgan gave the biggest "yes" he had ever given in the history of the show. When Simon Cowell called her a tiger and said she could go back to the village with her head held high with three yeses, she threw her arms up in the air, stomped her feet on the ground, and pranced offstage. An international sensation had been born. Nine days later, the video of Susan Boyle's performance had gone viral on YouTube. By 2013 she had sold over 19 million albums.

Susan Boyle's fame proves that the world not only recognizes, but also rewards those who find and express their *muchness*. What made Susan Boyle's performance demand a standing ovation and earn the greatest "YES" of the show's history? Some might argue that it was her talent, and others might say it was her unique character that seemingly didn't match her powerhouse mezzo-soprano voice. But arguably, Susan Boyle isn't any different than you or me. In fact, she faces challenges beyond what many of us could imagine. A childhood diagnosis of brain damage was revised in 2013 to Asperger's Syndrome, a condition on the autism spectrum. Despite her challenges in social settings, Boyle is the subject of a feel-good inspirational story that proves anyone can find and express their *muchness*. So what exactly did she do or have in her expression of herself that made everyone who watched stand up and take notice?

The answer lies in her shaking hips and proud strut, her confidence and choice of song, her stomping feet and upraised arms. When Boyle strutted onto stage and shook her hips at the judges, she asserted a confidence and ease in her state of being. Her spunk coupled with the lyrics of the song *I Dreamed a Dream* indicated a mental state of passion and a belief in herself and her dream that spilled over into the audience. Upon receiving the news that she received three resounding yeses, she stomped her feet on the ground and raised her arms high, making herself not only bigger and taller, but more grounded and solid, almost as if she were symbolically stepping into her *muchness*.

Body + Mind + Spirit = MUCHNESS

Boyle's performance was an example of ideal body/mind/spirit alignment. While she held her body in proud posture, she kept a mental attitude of confidence and even sang lyrics to a song that supported her mental intention. The third element of the equation, spirit, lies in her skill as a vocalist to breathe fully. The word *spirit* comes from the Latin root word *spiritus*, which means "breath." As a vocal singer, Boyle had practiced and mastered her ability to breathe fully, and expressed her breath, her spirit, through her singing. An analysis of her *Britain's Got Talent* performance reveals that Susan Boyle's body posture, mental attitude, and spirit breath is the perfect integration of body/mind/spirit. The result was obvious: *MUCHNESS.*

Susan Boyle's *I Dreamed a Dream* performance is only one of many examples of people living and expressing their *muchness.* Other examples might include: Martin Luther King Jr.'s *I Have a Dream* speech, President John F. Kennedy's Inaugural Address, or Steve Jobs' Stanford University Commencement Speech. Lesser known examples can be found in the stories of everyday people. On the show *Undercover Boss* hard-working people do their seemingly unpleasant jobs with *muchness.* In 2009, the father of a precocious toddler named Jessica posted a video of his daughter shouting affirmations of *muchness* to herself in the bathroom mirror, and the video went viral. Soul Pancake, a website (www.soulpancake.com) that makes and posts various feel-good videos, posted a video of complete strangers in a ball pit on the street talking about life's big questions, and deep connections and sharing of *muchness* resulted. *Muchness* is everywhere, including right inside yourself. You just need to open your eyes to it.

The word muchness was common during Shakespearean times. It means "the quality or state of being great."

Identifying those who live and share their *muchness* is easy. They evoke standing ovations when they speak. They make you smile. They inspire others to want to take action and believe in the seemingly impossible. They give you a warm feeling in your heart and a fiery passion in your belly. They seem happier than the average individual. Like Susan Boyle, these individuals hold an aura of *muchness.*

The Looking Glass

Can Susan Boyle look in the mirror and see her *muchness* aura? What exactly does that aura of *muchness* look like? It is hard to define as it holds a sort of elusive "you know it when you see it" energy. A psychic who has practiced reading auras as colors and lights that surround people may be able to define the aura of *muchness* more specifically. However, how is it that those of us who cannot see colors and energies, auras, can instantly recognize when someone is fully standing (or sitting) in their *muchness*? Why is it that we can believe that we all have the ability to access our own *muchness*, as well as the ability to see the *muchness* in others even when they aren't showing it fully, but we can't see or access this *muchness* consistently in ourselves? Why do children seem to spout their *muchness* more naturally, and the older we get, the more our *muchness* hides like a cat under the bed? Why can we occasionally access our *muchness* in random moments, but other times it seems to be locked behind the tiny door at the bottom of Wonderland's rabbit hole? What can we do to consciously evoke our *muchness* on a consistent basis?

Forgetting that when I was ten years old I had tucked my own *muchness* safely away in the sock drawer of my psyche with the tights I never wanted to wear because they were too itchy, I've spent the better part of thirty years asking these questions in an effort to find my *muchness* again. I have always wondered why, like the lion and the tin man and the scarecrow of *The Wizard of Oz*, we search for the courage and the heart and the brain that we have inside ourselves all along. I'm guilty of it myself. I was teased as a child for wearing the wrong brand of jeans, for needing thick glasses, for being the poorest kid in a wealthy suburban community. I was even hassled for being too smart and breaking the grading curve in math class. I learned to be ashamed of my four eyes and my poor fashion sense while I pretended to not know the answer when the teacher called on me. As I grew older, I learned that everyone, absolutely everyone, has stories of hiding their *muchness* like I did and often still do.

My desire to answer these elusive questions about *muchness* has led me to go about my life sporting a rather stylish pair of rose colored glasses that help me to look underneath the wounds and scars of the people I meet and see the precious gem underneath that just requires a little spit shine. As a result, I have this gift (which sometimes feels like a curse) to see the *muchness* of every single person I meet. I can relate to Kermit the Frog who adores his Miss Piggy for her ambition and passion to defend what she loves despite her irrational temper tantrums and fits of jealousy and insecurity. I feel his pain when he sings *It's Not Easy Being Green*, yet I find his greenness rather beautiful.

While some might say that my ability to see colors and lights around people is a psychic gift, the truth is that I have just spent the better part of thirty years practicing and developing a keen sense of observation. I pay attention to body language, especially as a result of my work as a yoga instructor. As a writer, I am acutely aware of and intrigued by figurative language, word choice, tone, and mood. For the last several years I have made a career as a spiritual coach. I sit with people one-on-one as they tell me their stories. I get to meet the most fascinating people (absolutely everyone in this world is fascinating) and help them discover, or rather, remember the shiny brightness inside them that I observe through these ever so subtle cues. I watch their body language, take note of their facial expressions, and listen carefully for cues in their tone of voice and diction. I am so lucky! On a daily basis, I get to show these radiant people their *muchness* in the reflection of my rose colored glasses. I dream a dream of one day providing everyone I meet with a looking glass of their very own that they can use to remind themselves of their *muchness.*

The MOZI EXPERIENCE is that looking glass. It is a step by step series of exercises, a methodical system of body/mind/spirit practices that you can incorporate into your everyday life to remind you in just a matter of seconds, in the moment, of your *muchness* and help you to behave and express yourself as your TRUE SELF in any scenario, situation or circumstance. Like anything, through consistent practice, your body can develop the muscle memory of body/mind/spirit integration so that living your *muchness* and expressing your true self becomes more automatic.

Body - Posture

I first discovered the power of body movement and language over my moods and emotions when I suffered clinical depression in my early twenties. I felt like my *muchness* had been taken hostage by a big ugly demon that lived deep inside a black hole that had consumed my heart. In an effort to get off the anti-depressants, which produced side effects that were almost worse than the depression itself, I began a rigorous workout regimen. I was able to wean myself off the drugs through an addiction to cardio-kickboxing, weight-training, and step aerobics. I literally beat my depression demon into submission every day, and I needed to be in peak physical form to do so. While I was extremely strong, I was not calm. I kept my depression demon knocked out, but my *muchness* (which I have since learned requires a balance of strength and calm) stayed hidden inside the folds my boxing glove wraps. While I was no longer depressed, I wasn't exactly happy. My kickboxing ferocity intimidated even my own *muchness*.

Then, one day my weight training coach suggested I try yoga, and everything changed. With each posture, I felt both strong and calm. I left the class feeling true happiness, and I tasted the delicious flavor of *muchness* that I hadn't experienced since childhood. My keen sense of observation noticed that the students in the class exhibited a greater expression of their *muchness* during the practice. I traded in my boxing gloves and dumbbells for a yoga mat and embarked on an intensive study of *muchness*.

Since the human body is the vehicle through which we all experience life, I figured that *muchness* is rooted in using the body as it was designed to be used, to its greatest efficiency. Yoga helped me to find that mechanical efficiency. While weight lifting and kickboxing were exercises in exertion, endurance, and effort, yoga taught me to use effort AND relax. My practice showed me that doing less always resulted in feeling more. Feeling more always resulted in feeling *muchier*. I always walked out of my yoga class feeling more of my *muchness*. Looking back through my fitness journals and comparing my comments during my aerobics and weight training days to my yoga days, I discovered that one hour of yoga produced better feelings than I could attain with four hours of aerobics and weight training.

I became a sort of mad yoga scientist. I attended intensely crazy yoga bootcamps, twisted my own body up into knots, and crashed on my face way too many times while attempting what I now call stupid human tricks. I filled dozens of journals documenting my practice and my experiences. Scientifically, I came to understand that putting my body in optimum alignment, specifically the alignment of the spine, provides a more direct passageway between the body and the brain. When I put myself in a certain position, for example, mimicking a warrior, my body sent the message to my brain that I need to be warrior-like, and my brain responded by sending hormones into my system to make me FEEL warrior-like. The more aligned my body was in the posture, the more warrior-like I felt, as if the message from my body to brain was clearer and the absorption of the warrior hormones into my system was more efficient with better postural alignment. I studied the science of hormones and the nervous system, and experienced this science in my own body on my mat and documented the benefits in my journal.

Three years into my yoga practice, I started teaching yoga. My yoga students became my lab rats as I paid close attention to posture and alignment as body language of the inner state of my students. I took copious notes and compiled thousands of case study files of students who were eager to let me sit with them one-on-one and listen to their stories.

In working with people who claimed they weren't flexible or strong enough to do yoga or had various injuries, I had to adapt and bring the practice to its very fundamental foundation. My students couldn't twist into the pretzel poses or balance in the stupid human tricks I had practiced at retreats on the beaches in Mexico. I discovered that stupid human tricks were just that, stupid and unnecessary. When my students complained of what they couldn't do, I took their issues into my own body and performed the poses with the modifications I gave them to see if the effects were the same. I discovered that the effects were, in fact, better if I took the modifications AND focused on my breath and spinal alignment. As a result, my own practice has evolved. Today, I literally roll out of bed onto my yoga mat. Still in my pajamas, I breathe my body through twenty minutes of simple poses, focusing entirely on breath and spinal alignment rather than the pose as it appears in pictures. Referencing my journal testimonies, I can argue that I am in much better health now than I was when I was doing pretzel poses and stupid human tricks in overheated sweaty rooms.

So, I started teaching the concept that less is more and brought my students' focus to breath and basic fundamental spinal alignment. Their *muchness* becomes even more *muchier*! One day, while teaching a teacher training class, I saw this *muchier muchness* appear in my students' bodies, and I said, "Wow, you are all full of *muchness*! Let's just hold this pose for a moment and affirm your MUCHNESS!" And right before my eyes, the room filled with a dozen Susan Boyles singing *I Dreamed a Dream* in their bodies. I was blown away when I experimented with giving my students simple mindful affirmations to link to their focused breath and simple alignment.

After nearly a decade as mad yoga scientist, tens of thousands of hours on my mat, thousands of pages of notes and journals, and with the support of thousands of willing students in my laboratory, my research has boiled down to the simple theory that good posture linked to breath and mental intention makes the brain and the body function better, producing the effect of *muchness.*

The MOZI EXPERIENCE teaches the magic and science of yoga without the crazy pretzel positions or the stupid human tricks.

For MOZI, you don't need to be flexible or strong, wear fancy yoga clothes or even able to sit cross legged with your hands in your lap. The MOZI EXPERIENCE employs simple body posture to activate the intelligence of your physiology to do what it is meant to do. It's not complicated. It's practical.

Mind – Education

When I was young, I loved school. While I enjoyed every class, my passion for language and literature emerged when I won a creative writing competition in third grade. I became obsessed with words, poetry and figurative language as a means to describe what went on in my creative imagination. I loved language mostly because, aside from the rules of grammar, there were no wrong answers in analyzing poetry and prose. I relished the idea that literature gave everyone the right to their own opinions and provided the means for people to express themselves in full honesty without the fear of getting the answer wrong. Rather, literature challenged me to dig inside myself about how I felt about something I'd read and be able to defend my opinion, to assert my inner beliefs and values. In other words, studying literature was a way to dig into the *muchness* I had hidden, and creative writing was a way to express it.

I took Latin in high school because I wanted to really understand the evolution of language. I enjoyed learning Latin vocabulary because it gave me a better understanding of English vocabulary, such as the fact that the English word *spirit* comes from the Latin word *spiritus* which means breath. Another significant example to me, the word *education* comes from the Latin root *educare*, which translates to "to draw forth from within." In other words, to educate, is to bring out what already exists inside. The day I learned the etymology of the word *educate* I decided I wanted to be an educator when I grew up, to help people pull wisdom out from within themselves. A decade later, my yoga teacher shared the etymology of the word *educate* with the class, and TA-DA, two of my loves, language and yoga, merged.

As much as I loved school as a child, college and grad school were my playground. I triple majored in creative writing, literary studies, and education, eventually earning a Master's Degree in teaching. If my advisors had let me, I would've added Latin as well. At a small, private liberal arts college in southern Wisconsin, I became obsessed with integrating what I learned in my general education courses with what I was studying in my majors. My personal journals were filled with diagrams and essays linking what I learned about Pythagoras in math class to what I learned from Ptolemy in astronomy class to what I learned about the metrics and tempo of Shakespearean iambic pentameter in my poetry classes. In short, college not only provided me with a vocation as a high school English teacher, but it taught me one very big lesson that I take with me in every part of life: absolutely everything is connected.

One thing I did for myself in my journals through my college years was to summarize what I had learned in a course in one simple sentence. For example, for astronomy class, I wrote, "The universe is really big and magical beyond imagination." For Survey of Women's Literature I wrote, "Women are complicated and brilliant and very powerful." For Introduction to Mathematical Thinking I wrote, "Mathematicians are extremely creative." I call this practice my "take-away," and I have employed it in every class I have ever taught, high school and yoga. As a teacher, I continue to write what I learn in teaching in take-aways, and I often ask my students to do the same. It's an exercise in affirming what it is that was drawn out from within through the learning process. In essence, a take-away is the mindful affirmation applied to the practice. In the MOZI EXPERIENCE, take-aways are both provided as simple affirmations during the exercises and extracted from students in the interactive assignments, journals, and surveys.

After years of teaching and thousands of take-aways, the take-away I have for what I have learned about teaching and education is **"students learn best when lessons are kept simple and personal."** In other words, the best way to draw the wisdom out from within my students is to provide a very simple road map for them to navigate themselves. In order to do this, no matter what I teach, I follow a few very specific rules in my teaching

- Keep content basic and *simple*
- Provide many opportunities for *repetition and practice*
- Encourage *interaction* among students
- Foster *independence* so students eventually don't need the teacher
- Support *personalization* so students can apply what they learn to their own lives

While everyone has something to share with the world, and thus is a natural teacher, I have discovered that the majority of yoga teacher trainings produce instructors and teachers, not educators. The industry is filled with thousands of qualified and talented individuals who deliver entertaining instruction and quality content, but for the most part, they do not educate. They lecture and instruct as a means of installing information in the student, but they do not often draw the wisdom out from within their students. I believe that while the yoga industry has boomed in the last decade, a huge population is still not exposed to the magic of body-mind-spirit integration through yoga because the industry (while it has excellent instructors) is lacking in quality education.

The MOZI EXPERIENCE seeks to provide a quality educational experience to anyone and everyone who wants to benefit from body-mind-spirit integration.

The MOZI EXPERIENCE employs the best practices of learning as simplicity, repetition and practice, interaction, personalization, and independence. You don't need to be flexible, or strong, or confident enough to go to a yoga studio. You don't even need to invest in any trendy yoga apparel or be able to quiet the mind and sit in meditation. The MOZI EXPERIENCE is designed to educate, to draw forth from within, all the wisdom you already have and remind you of the strength and flexibility and confidence you already possess inside you. Through mindful affirmations (takeaways) linked to body posture and breath, the MOZI EXPERIENCE reveals the *muchness* you already are.

Spirit - Breath

Breath is spirit. If you don't believe me, just try holding your breath for a half a second longer than you are comfortable and see what happens. As I have already said, the word for breath in Latin comes from the same root as the word Spirit. *Spirit* in Latin means "he or she breathes." Breath is energy. Breath is life. Without breath, everything goes flat and eventually dies. The human body requires energy to survive. If you stop breathing for too long, you die. It's that simple. Without breath, the spirit leaves the body. 80-90% of the energy you receive in your body each day comes from breath, leaving only 10-20% of our energetic fuel to come from food. This makes sense because we breathe continually all day long, but we only eat food in small portions of our day. Breath is spirit.

While I already knew the power and magic of breath as spirit through my yoga practice, my real understanding of breath as spirit came to me through an intensive study of the natural elements of earth, water, fire, nature, and mineral. In 2006 I met an African shaman who travels the world teaching westerners the spiritual wisdoms of his indigenous tribe in West Africa. During an intensive two-year shamanic study program, I learned that the five elements are symbolic of five essential qualities of life: earth for grounding, water for flow, fire for passion, nature for connection, and mineral for expression. The one thing that all five elements are completely dependent upon is air, or breath, OR SPIRIT. In effort to understand these elements better and how to integrate their spiritual wisdoms into my body, I moved my yoga practice from the comfort of my climate-controlled home into the world of the glorious outdoors.

Going outside to get a breath of fresh air took on a whole new meaning when I planted my bare feet in mountain pose on the earthy soil of a river bank. My shaman teacher taught me to bury my feet in the ground to feel safe, fill my pockets with stones to feel the vibration of my bones, wash my pains away in the river, burn my fears in a fire, and dance to the songs of birds. In accordance with my college take-away that everything is connected, I instinctively applied what I was learning about the five natural elements in my shamanic study to my yoga practice. I discovered that, like everything else, the five natural elements exist *inside* me. I could *feel* them activate in my body through the simple practices of yoga, and more so when I set breath to intention to posture.

> The MOZI EXPERIENCE is the practice of moving your muchness through your body with your breath.

How to MOZI?

So how exactly does one MOZI? You've already started. You picked up this book and you've read this far. Keep reading. This book is the MOZI EXPERIENCE Basic Training. In Basic Training you will learn five three-second body/mind/spirit techniques that are simple, realistic, practical, and applicable to everyday life as tools to remember your true self. You will learn to:

- Stand Your Ground
- Go With the Flow
- Access Your Strength
- Relate to Others
- Speak Your Mind

But the MOZI EXPERIENCE isn't just words in a book, it's a full immersion experience. There's so much more to MOZI than what you will read here. I encourage you to immerse yourself in these teachings, to incorporate the practices in your daily life. Allow the process to coax your muchness out in the open. The more you put into your MOZI experience, the more you'll get out of yourself. Yet, you need not dive into these teachings with intense fervor. Instead, I encourage you to mosey through them like a leisurely stroll. Take them as fast or slow as you like, just be sure to fully enjoy every step of the process, like Mozi the dog stopping to touch his nose to my cheek.

My high school literature teacher once said that the best way to read a book is to read the whole thing in one sitting. Naively, I read all fourteen hundred pages of Victor Hugo's unabridged *Les Misérables* over Thanksgiving weekend of my senior year. Talk about dreaming a dream! I don't recommend reading historical tomes in one sitting because I not only alienated my extended family on a major holiday, but suffered sleep deprivation, temporary mal-nutrition, disorientation, and nightmares of being forced into prostitution during the French Revolution.

On the other hand, I don't blame you if you devour this book in one sitting. I actually encourage it. I wrote it to be a very easy read so that it doesn't end up on the bottom shelf with all the other half-finished books of the world. The high school English teacher in me encourages you to go back and re-read, re-do, re-view, and re-evaluate the chapters of this book several times and often. Mark it up. Make notes in the margins. Underline passages and highlight your own notes. Lather. Rinse. Repeat. Mozi, the Great Dane, returned to me several times that day, each time, showing me a slightly different side of himself. The more you repeat the content of a lesson, the more likely you are to remember it. The more you practice an exercise, the more likely you are to develop it into a habit. Each time you work your way through the content, you will discover new things about yourself. My hope is that after you make your way through this book several times, eventually the words you write in it will far out number the words I wrote. You see, writing your own thoughts helps personalize the experience for you and make it more real and more YOU.

Unlike the effects of immersing myself for three days in the beautifully written words but incredible darkness of Victor Hugo's prose, the effects of completely drowning myself in The MOZI Experience completely changed me. The word *change* is somewhat deceptive because I don't think I really changed as much as I *remembered* who I was all along. I speak from personal experience that employing these simple practices over and over and over made me be more ME. I stopped pretending to be what other people expected, or what I thought other people wanted me to be. These exercises made me find a more natural and easy way to go about my life without pretention and effort, but with ease and freedom. On a physical level, these practices helped me learn how to use my body more efficiently. On a mental and emotional level, these practices helped me respond to the everyday challenges in my life more appropriately. While the only thing I remember about *Les Misérables* is the names of the characters were Jean Valjean and Cosette, the content of the MOZI Experience is knitted into the very fabric of every muscle and tissue in my body, mind, and spirit.

CHAPTER TWO

Breathe

"For breath is life, and if you breathe well you will live long on earth."
~Sanskrit Proverb

Theresa, a mother of four children under the age of ten and wife to a husband on disability due to post-traumatic stress from serving in Iraq, owned her own private therapy practice where she counseled dozens of clients with a wide range of challenges. Needless to say, Theresa lived a high stress life. Theresa came to my yoga class looking for a way to relax. She also wanted to learn stress management tools to provide to her clients. One day in class I suggested that students try taking deep breaths every time they came to a stop sign or stoplight on their drive home. A few weeks later, Theresa gave me an amazing testimonial of what this little exercise did for her. The first day she noticed she was less anxious about getting home to feed her kids. The second day she noticed she wasn't as short-tempered or angry with her family. The third day she realized she had gone three days without her usual after-work glass of red wine. The fourth day she discovered she was enjoying her family time more than usual.

The simple practice of focused breathing at stoplights was having a significant impact on her life. Breathing deeply at stoplights became habit to Theresa. She had even learned how to ignore the little honks of cars behind her when she didn't immediately put her foot on the gas when a light turned green because she hadn't finished her breath. One evening, she had not yet finished her long exhale when the light turned green, and as she had done many times before, she took the extra couple seconds to finish her exhale. In those moments, a semi-truck came barreling through the intersection against his own red light. If she hadn't waited to finish her breath, a tragic crash would have occurred, and she would likely have died. Stopping to breathe didn't just improve her quality of life, that day it *saved* her life.

You breathe all day long. Every breath provides your body with energy in the form of oxygen that is circulated through your entire body via your bloodstream. On the other hand, you only eat at certain times a day, and when you eat, your body must consume energy in order to convert food into energy. Therefore, 80-90% of energy comes from breath while only 10-20% of energy comes from food. The more you breathe, with better efficiency and fullness, the more energy you have to supply your daily life activities.

Benefits of Focused Breathing

- Lowers the heart rate
- Decreases blood pressure
- Relaxes muscle tension
- Cleans, filters, warms and humidifies air
- Calms the nervous system
- Oxygenates the body
- Decreases infections and bacteria
- Improves immune function
- Removes toxins from the body
- Aids in digestion
- Enhances circulation
- Quiets the mind
- Calms the nerves
- Decreases anxiety
- Improves focus
- Slows the thoughts
- Promotes clarity
- Increases awareness
- Stabilizes emotions
- Releases tension and stress
- Lowers impulse reactivity
- Provides time to process a situation

Focused Breathing Pre-Test

Answer the following questions based on how you feel RIGHT NOW.

I feel stressed.
Agree   5   4   3   2   1   0   Disagree

I feel focused, aware, and able to act with purpose.
Agree   5   4   3   2   1   0   Disagree

I feel relaxed, open, calm, and aware.
Agree   5   4   3   2   1   0   Disagree

I feel physically open, flexible, and free.
Agree   5   4   3   2   1   0   Disagree

Journal

How aware are you of your breathing patterns? How deep is your natural breath? How full is your natural breath? How long is your natural breath? When do you stop to take deep breaths? When should you stop to take deep breaths? How do you feel when you get a long, full, deep breath? When in your life do you think you could benefit from becoming more aware of your breathing?

Focused Breathing Technique

1. Take a deep breath and pay attention to the depth, volume, tone, and quality of your breath.
2. Hold your hand up in front of your nose and mouth as if it were a mirror that you are going to fog up with your breath.
3. Breathe in AND out of your mouth as if you are fogging up the mirror of your hand. Pay attention to the feeling and sound at the back of your throat.
4. Drop your hand and close your mouth, and continue to breathe as if fogging up the mirror.
5. Try to keep that feeling at the back of your throat. The feeling and sound will be like a subtle snoring sensation and make sound like an ocean inside your skull. Be sure to keep that feeling and sound on BOTH the inhalation and the exhalation.
6. Take 5-10 more focused breaths like this. Pay attention to the depth, volume, tone, and quality of your breath.
7. Return to normal breathing. (Focused breathing is a practice to help you focus in the moment and is not meant to be sustained all day long.)
8. Make a few notes here of what differences you notice from before employing the focused breathing technique to after.

Homework

Practice this Focused Breathing Technique every time you come to a stop during your day: at stop signs, at stoplights, while waiting in line, while waiting on hold, while taking a break from work, before switching to a new task, etc. Make a few notes here about how you feel at the end of the day after practicing this Focused Breathing throughout the day.

Focused Breathing Post-Test

For best results, practice this exercise for a day or longer before taking the post-test. Then, answer the following questions based on how you feel RIGHT NOW.

I feel stressed.
Agree   5   4   3   2   1   0   Disagree

I feel focused, aware, and able to act with purpose.
Agree   5   4   3   2   1   0   Disagree

I feel relaxed, open, calm, and aware.
Agree   5   4   3   2   1   0   Disagree

I feel physically open, flexible, and free.
Agree   5   4   3   2   1   0   Disagree

Compare your answers here to the answers you gave in the pre-test. Make notes here as to the differences:

Questions for Review

Body – when you take a long, slow, focused breath, what effects do you notice in your body? Be specific and include which body parts you feel affected and what the effect was.

Mind – when you take a long, slow, focused breath, what shift do you experience in your thoughts and ability to process information? Be specific. Give an example of something you were thinking and how it changed with focused breath.

Spirit – when you take a long slow focused breath, what shift do you experience in your mood, feelings, and emotions? Be specific.

CHAPTER THREE

Stand Your Ground

"Be sure to put your feet in the right place, then stand firm."
~Abraham Lincoln

When my little brother David was seven years old, he came home from a Cub Scouts meeting where he learned a simple martial arts technique. As the baby in the family who was soft-spoken, he often felt like he was the pushover of the family. One by one, he challenged us to pick him up. At just over sixty pounds, he was by far the lightest member of the family. I was eleven at the time, and tried first, but I couldn't budge his feet off the ground. Our older brother, Eric, who was fifteen, went next and was also unsuccessful. Then Mom, and finally Dad both failed in their attempts. When we all asked him to tell him us how he did it, he simply said, "It's a Jedi-mind trick I learned in Cub Scouts today." Mom told us later that she'd heard that the guest presenter at his Cub Scouts meeting was an aikido master who shared with the boys some of the techniques of the ancient martial art.

Years later, as a young adult, employing this simple technique became a habit in David's life. Rather than being the little brother we used to toss around, we now see him as the man whose mind and body cannot be moved when he commits himself to something. Anytime he wants to assert his opinion in an argument, refuse to do something someone requests of him, or even get what he wants, he stands his ground. As a lover of surfing, he appreciates the value of being flexible and isn't completely stubborn, yet at the same time, when David's mind is made up, David's mind is made up.

David's story isn't an example of super-human powers. With a little practice you may be able to become unmovable as well. Simply follow Abraham Lincoln's advice and apply the MOZI Stand Your Ground technique by putting your feet in the right place and standing firm, set a mindful intention of being unable to be moved, and breathe consciously into that intention. That's all David does, and it's worked for him for nearly thirty years.

Benefits of Stand Your Ground

- Improves stability
- Increases leg strength
- Supports better balance
- Decreases pain in the feet, legs, knees, and ankles
- Increases awareness of the body mechanics of your lower body (feet, ankles, knees, calves, thighs)
- Strengthens the internal thigh muscles
- Enhances feelings of safety and security
- Promotes ability to stay committed
- Develops determination and perseverance
- Decreases anxiety and worry
- Provides stillness
- Calms agitation
- Quiets nervousness
- Improves ability to handle stress in the areas of home, health, family, stability, and basic needs

Stand Your Ground Pre-Test

Answer the following questions based on how you feel RIGHT NOW.

I feel pain in my legs, knees, ankles, and/or feet.
Agree   5   4   3   2   1   0   Disagree

I feel safe, secure and supported.
Agree   5   4   3   2   1   0   Disagree

I feel capable of handling stress in the areas of family, home, health, and finances.
Agree   5   4   3   2   1   0   Disagree

I feel able to adjust and compensate when I am shaken off my ground.
Agree   5   4   3   2   1   0   Disagree

I feel stable, and able to stand my ground.
Agree   5   4   3   2   1   0   Disagree

Journal

Write about times in your life when standing your ground and having more stability and foundation would be helpful. Write about times in your life when you felt you were knocked off your ground, pushed-over, the rug was pulled out from underneath you, or you were cut off at the knees. Include both physical ailments of the feet and legs and metaphorical situations of being dropped to your knees.

Stand Your Ground Technique

1. Place your feet hip width distance apart, with your heels slightly out so that when you look down, your feet are parallel to each other like two number ones.
2. Push down through all parts of your foot: your heel, your big toe mound, and the pinky toe side of your foot.
3. Engage your inner thighs. (It helps to squeeze a yoga block, or even a tissue box between them). Notice that when you stand like this the sensations are different than when you just stand normally.
4. Take a few Focused Breaths.
5. Say to yourself "I am solid, firm, grounded, and stable."
6. Take 5-10 more focused breaths like this. Pay attention to how safe and secure and stable you feel in your body, especially your legs and feet.
7. Make a few notes here of what differences you notice from before employing the Stand Your Ground technique to after.

Homework

Practice this Stand Your Ground Technique every time you are standing still during your day: brushing your teeth, doing dishes, waiting in line, cooking, checking out at a store, etc. Make a few notes here about how you feel at the end of the day after practicing this Stand Your Ground technique throughout the day.

Stand Your Ground Post-Test

For best results, practice this exercise for a day or longer before taking the post-test. Then, answer the following questions based on how you feel RIGHT NOW.

I feel pain in my legs, knees, ankles, and/or feet.
Agree   5   4   3   2   1   0   Disagree

I feel safe, secure and supported.
Agree   5   4   3   2   1   0   Disagree

I feel capable of handling stress in the areas of family, home, health, and finances.
Agree   5   4   3   2   1   0   Disagree

I feel able to adjust and compensate when I am shaken off my ground.
Agree   5   4   3   2   1   0   Disagree

I feel stable, and able to stand my ground.
Agree   5   4   3   2   1   0   Disagree

Compare your answers here to the answers you gave in the pre-test. Make notes here as to the differences:

Questions for Review

Body – when you practice Stand Your Ground alignment, what effects do you notice in your body? Be specific and include which body parts you feel affected and what the effect was.

Mind – when you practice "Stand Your Ground" affirmations, what shift do you experience in your thoughts and ability to process information? Be specific. Give an example of something you were thinking and how it changed with Stand Your Ground.

Spirit – when you Stand Your Ground, what shift do you experience in your mood, feelings, and emotions? Be specific.

CHAPTER FOUR

Go With the Flow

"Water is the driving force of all nature."
~Lao Tzu

At seventy years old, my Grandma Florence could bend at the waist with her legs straight and place her hands flat on the floor a couple inches behind her heels. When her doctor informed her that she needed a hip replacement, she asked him two questions. First, how long does an artificial hip last? And second, could she continue to do her African dance aerobics twice a week? When he told her that the hip would last about fifteen years, she informed him that she would likely be having it done twice because she planned on living to be one hundred years old. When the doctor told her that flexibility would be limited in the new hip but that she could still dance with reasonable modifications, she said that she has been making modifications all her life, as she was the queen of flexibility.

Grandma Florence's ability to adjust to circumstances in her life was reflected in her personality as well as her physical flexibility. She could mimic the moves of a giraffe and gazelle in her dance class in the morning, and by evening prepare a five course meal for her husband's business associates on just a few hours notice. Her physical flexibility in dance class allowed her to be mentally and emotionally flexible when her plans for the day were changed unexpectedly. In all aspects of the phrase, she was able to go with the flow of life.

"Go With the Flow" is probably one of the most commonly used phrases to describe how people would like to approach a situation. The opposite, "swimming upstream" or "going against the current" is hardly a desirable course of action. As most of the earth is made up of water, as is the human body, and water flows, going with the flow is an easier and more natural way to live. Learning to use your body like water coupled with focused breathing and mindful affirmations will help you Go With the Flow and find your own flexibility in both body and life. While you aren't likely to be able to fold in half and put your hands flat on the floor like Grandma Florence (she may just have had super-flexible-human powers) this exercise will improve your overall flexibility.

Benefits of Go With the Flow

- Improves flexibility
- Increases range of motion
- Supports joint health and function
- Promotes ease in movement
- Lowers risk of injury
- Stretches and elongates muscles
- Decreases "klutziness"
- Supports letting go
- Decreases perfectionism
- Inhibits over-controlling tendencies
- Lessens obsessive and compulsive behaviors
- Helps in facing situations that are out of one's control
- Promotes creativity
- Produces a sense of peace and calm
- Teaches an acceptance of the unknown or unexpected
- Creates a sense of freedom
- Quiets anxiety and worry
- Teaches the power of observation

Go With the Flow Pre-Test

Answer the following questions based on how you feel RIGHT NOW

I feel pain in my pelvis, hips, or other joints.
Agree   5   4   3   2   1   0   Disagree

I feel happy and joyful.
Agree   5   4   3   2   1   0   Disagree

I feel capable of handling stress in the areas of workload, control, addictions, and cravings.
Agree   5   4   3   2   1   0   Disagree

I feel able to adjust and compensate when plans and circumstances change unexpectedly.
Agree   5   4   3   2   1   0   Disagree

I feel flexible and able to go with the flow.
Agree   5   4   3   2   1   0   Disagree

Journal

Write about times in your life when going with the flow and having more flexibility, creativity, and freedom would be helpful. Write about times in your life when you felt you were out of control or challenged by your ability to control external circumstances. Include both physical ailments of the hips, joints, pelvis and reproductive system and metaphorical situations of being stuck or overwhelmed.

Go With the Flow Technique

1. Begin focused breathing.
2. Affirm to yourself, "I am flexible and can go with the flow of whatever happens."
3. As you continue your focused breath, shake out your entire body (like doing the hokey pokey and shaking it all about).
4. Let yourself be silly and feel goofy. The benefits will outweigh the embarrassment.
5. Affirm again, "I am flexible and can go with the flow of whatever happens."
6. Make a few notes here of what differences you notice from before employing the Go With the Flow technique to after.

Homework

Practice this Go With the Flow Technique every time you are around water during your day: every time you go to the bathroom, doing dishes or cleaning, whenever you wash your hands, while in the shower, anytime you get caught in the rain or snow, etc. Make a few notes here about how you feel at the end of the day after practicing this Go With the Flow technique throughout the day.

Go With the Flow Post-Test

For best results, practice this exercise for a day or longer before taking the post-test. Then, answer the following questions based on how you feel RIGHT NOW.

I feel pain in my pelvis, hips, or other joints.
Agree   5   4   3   2   1   0   Disagree

I feel happy and joyful.
Agree   5   4   3   2   1   0   Disagree

I feel capable of handling stress in the areas of workload, control, addictions, and cravings.
Agree   5   4   3   2   1   0   Disagree

I feel able to adjust and compensate when plans and circumstances change unexpectedly.
Agree   5   4   3   2   1   0   Disagree

I feel flexible and able to go with the flow.
Agree   5   4   3   2   1   0   Disagree

Compare your answers here to the answers you gave in the pretest. Make notes here as to the differences:

Questions for Review

Body – when you practice Go With the Flow alignment, what effects do you notice in your body? Be specific and include which body parts you feel affected and what the effect was.

Mind – when you practice "Go With the Flow" affirmations, what shift do you experience in your thoughts and ability to process information? Be specific. Give an example of something you were thinking and how it changed with Go With the flow.

Spirit – when you Go With the Flow, what shift do you experience in your mood, feelings, and emotions? Be specific.

CHAPTER FIVE

Access Your Strength

"The mind is not a vessel to be filled but a fire to be kindled."
~Plutarch

For ten years, I was a high school English teacher for some of the roughest students in the building. I communicated more with my students' parole officers than I did their parents. At five foot six and weighing less than 120 pounds, I was tiny compared to most of my students, and many of them were more than twice my size. Yet, I had earned their respect in such a way that the shop teacher often asked me to chaperone his field trips because his kids listened to me better than they did him. One morning, one of my beefiest students, Sam, got into a verbal altercation outside my classroom with another boy. When the bell rang to start class, I didn't hesitate to put myself between the boys, look up at Sam who was over a head taller than me and order him into the class-room. As soon as I shut the door behind me, the boy in the hallway shouted something that aggravated Sam. He responded by throw-ing me into the wall and charging out the door after the other boy. I momentarily lost consciousness. After coming to, I ran out the door to discover that a couple other teachers had intercepted the fight, and Sam was being taken to the principal's office. A few minutes later, the principal came to my classroom door and asked me to go to the office to deal with Sam while he watched my class. When I got to the principal's office, I found Sam in the fetal posi-tion on the floor sobbing like a baby, terrified that he had hurt his favorite teacher.

I was probably one of the physically smallest people who en-tered that school each day, yet I was able to assert one of the strongest personalities and commanded respect as if I were one of the largest. Whenever I stand in front of a classroom as an educa-tor, because it is what I love to do the most, I can access my strength and assert my *muchness*. Whether it be disciplining a ju-venile delinquent who had multiple charges of aggravated assault or guiding a class of one hundred athletes through a yoga se-quence, I feel strong in my core. The MOZI Access Your Strength exercise can help you find strength inside yourself, no matter your size or shape or genetic musculature.

Benefits of Access Your Strength

- Improves strength
- Increases muscle tone
- Supports balance
- Promotes ease in weight bearing activities
- Lowers risk of injury
- Stabilizes and supports joints
- Makes heavy lifting feel easier
- Teaches body awareness to work from your core
- Lowers your center of gravity
- Prevents low back pain and injury
- Strengthens and lengthens psoas muscles
- Connects upper body to lower body in functional unity
- Creates a feeling of 'upliftment'
- Regulates core temperature
- Detoxifies internal organs
- Supports health and function of digestive organs
- Increases confidence
- Improves self-esteem
- Ignites drive, passion, desire, and motivation
- Supports endurance and follow-through
- Produces a sense of courage and power
- Creates a sense of individual identity

Access Your Strength Pre-Test

Answer the following questions based on how you feel RIGHT NOW

<u>I feel pain in my core muscles and digestive system.</u>
Agree   5   4   3   2   1   0   Disagree

<u>I feel confident.</u>
Agree   5   4   3   2   1   0   Disagree

<u>I feel capable of handling stress in the areas of workload and victim/bully scenarios.</u>
Agree   5   4   3   2   1   0   Disagree

<u>I feel motivated, passionate, driven, focused and powerful in what I have to do.</u>
Agree   5   4   3   2   1   0   Disagree

<u>I feel strong, and able to access my strength.</u>
Agree   5   4   3   2   1   0   Disagree

Journal

Write about times in your life when accessing your strength and having more motivation, drive, power, confidence, and self-esteem would be helpful. Write about times in your life when you felt you gave away your power or were challenged in your ability to push through a challenge. Write about times you felt unmotivated, weak, tired, fatigued, or bored about something that should matter more. Include both physical ailments of the core strength and digestive system and metaphorical situations of feeling weak and victimized.

Access Your Strength Technique

1. Stand tall and put your hands on your belly.
2. Pull your bottom ribs and your hip bones slightly closer to-gether. Try putting your thumbs on your rib bones and your middle fingers on your hip bones and slightly hugging your belly muscles to bring the ribs and hips just a titch closer to each other.
3. Feel around the sides and back of your torso to make sure the space from your low ribs to your hips is even all the way around.
4. Keep this little self-hug (very soft embrace of your belly mus-cles) as you walk and notice how you walk taller and your gaze is lifted.
5. Begin focused breathing.
6. Affirm to yourself, "I confident, strong, and powerful."
7. Make a few notes here of what differences you notice from before employing the Access Your Strength technique to after.

Homework

Practice this Access Your Strength Technique every time you are walking during your day: from the car to the door, to the bathroom, walking your dog, shopping, anytime you move from one room to another, etc. Make a few notes here about how you feel at the end of the day after practicing this Access Your Strength technique throughout the day.

Access Your Strength Post-Test

For best results, practice this exercise for a day or longer before taking the post-test. Then, answer the following questions based on how you feel RIGHT NOW.

I feel pain in my core muscles and digestive system.
Agree   5   4   3   2   1   0   Disagree

I feel confident.
Agree   5   4   3   2   1   0   Disagree

I feel capable of handling stress in the areas of workload and victim/bully scenarios.
Agree   5   4   3   2   1   0   Disagree

I feel motivated, passionate, driven, focused and powerful in what I have to do.
Agree   5   4   3   2   1   0   Disagree

I feel strong, and able to access my strength.
Agree   5   4   3   2   1   0   Disagree

Compare your answers here to the answers you gave in the pre-test. Make notes here as to the differences:

Questions for Review

Body – when you practice Access Your Strength alignment, what effects do you notice in your body? Be specific and include which body parts you feel affected and what the effect was.

Mind – when you practice "Access Your Strength" affirmations, what shift do you experience in your thoughts and ability to process information? Be specific. Give an example of something you were thinking and how it changed with Access Your Strength.

Spirit – when you Access Your Strength, what shift do you experience in your mood, feelings, and emotions? Be specific.

CHAPTER SIX

Relate to Others

"If you want others to be happy, practice compassion.
If you want to be happy, practice compassion."
~Dalai Lama

I was having a very bad day. Like Alexander in Judith Viorst's classic children's book, I was having a terrible, horrible, no good, very bad day. Driving across Iowa in the dead of winter, I nearly slid off the road several times over black ice. Terrible. The contract job I was driving to texted to inform me enrollment was low and my paycheck could be cut in half. Horrible. The sandwich artist at Subway added onions when I specifically said "no onions." I hate onions. No good. My husband had asked for a divorce so that he could pursue a life as a celibate monk. Very, very bad, and just a tad bit weird.

So, when I walked up to the counter at a $59/night hotel, I didn't pay much attention to the clerk behind the counter. She, on the other hand, couldn't help but notice my tear-streaked face. When she gave me my room key, instead of just sliding it across the counter, she handed it to me with both hands, and held onto my hand as I grabbed it.

"Smile," she said, "I know it feels fake, but I just saw this video that said that if you fake smile, the muscles in your face tell your brain to make you feel happy for real. It can't hurt." She looked me right in the eye with a big smile and then winked as she withdrew her hands from mine. I couldn't help myself. It was like her smile traveled down her arms, through my hands, and planted itself right on my face.

This tiny exchange is a great example of the MOZI EXPERIENCE at work. This young woman had no clue what I was going through, but in that moment, she related to me and expressed her *muchness* in a tiny way, which in turn gave me permission to just be me. Even though in that moment, I was wounded and vulnerable, she made it okay for me to be me, as I really was, and that helped me remember just a tiny bit of my own *muchness*.

Benefits of Relate to Others

- Produces deeper, fuller breath
- Opens the lungs
- Improves circulation
- Creates openness in the body
- Relaxes shoulders and arms
- Releases tension in the upper back
- Improves symptoms from asthma, COPD, and other lung related issues
- Lowers blood pressure
- Slows pulse rate
- Quiets the mind
- Calms the nerves
- Decreases anxiety
- Improves focus
- Slows the thoughts
- Promotes clarity
- Increases awareness
- Stabilizes emotions
- Releases tension and stress
- Lowers impulse reactivity
- Creates a sense of openness
- Provides a feeling of space and freedom
- Stimulates compassion
- Decreases judgmental thoughts

Relate to Others Pre-Test

Answer the following questions based on how you feel RIGHT NOW.

I feel pain in my chest, arms, shoulder, elbows, hands, heart, and/or lungs.
Agree 5   4   3   2   1   0   Disagree

I have good relationships.
Agree 5   4   3   2   1   0   Disagree

I feel capable of handling stress in the areas of relationship and connection to others.
Agree 5   4   3   2   1   0   Disagree

I feel loving, compassionate, giving, and non-judgmental of others.
Agree 5   4   3   2   1   0   Disagree

I feel able and willing to receive when things are offered to me.
Agree 5   4   3   2   1   0   Disagree

Journal

Write about times in your life when relating to others through better access to your internal compassion, love, and ability to give and receive would be helpful. Write about times in your life when you felt you didn't see eye to eye with someone when it was important, were challenged in your ability to feel compassion for someone, or were unable to give or receive when you needed to. Write about times your felt like you had the weight of the world on your shoulders or you carried the burdens for others. Include both physical ailments of the chest and arms, respiratory and cardiovascular systems (heart and lungs) and metaphorical situations of feeling closed or broken hearted.

Relate to Others Technique

1. Stand or sit tall and put your thumbs in your armpits.
2. Lift your shoulders up, pull your shoulders back, drop your shoulders down, and release your thumbs from your armpits.
3. Feel your shoulder blades rest flat on your back as your breastbone opens.
4. Begin focused breathing.
5. Affirm to yourself, "I am open and compassionate toward others."
6. Make a few notes here of what differences you notice from before employing the Access Your Strength technique to after.

Homework

Practice this Relate to Others Technique every time you are about to engage in relationship during your day: answer the phone, make a call, write an email, listen to someone else speaking to you, etc. Make a few notes here about how you feel at the end of the day after practicing this Relate to Others technique throughout the day.

Relate to Others Post-Test

For best results, practice this exercise for a day or longer before taking the post-test. Then, answer the following questions based on how you feel RIGHT NOW.

I feel pain in my chest, arms, shoulder, elbows, hands, heart, and/or lungs.
Agree   5   4   3   2   1   0   Disagree

I have good relationships.
Agree   5   4   3   2   1   0   Disagree

I feel capable of handling stress in the areas of relationship and connection to others.
Agree   5   4   3   2   1   0   Disagree

I feel loving, compassionate, giving, and non-judgmental of others.
Agree   5   4   3   2   1   0   Disagree

I feel able and willing to receive when things are offered to me.
Agree   5   4   3   2   1   0   Disagree

Compare your answers here to the answers you gave in the pre-test. Make notes here as to the differences:

Questions for Review

Body – when you practice Relate to Others alignment, what effects do you notice in your body? Be specific and include which body parts you feel affected and what the effect was.

Mind – when you practice Relate to Others affirmations, what shift do you experience in your thoughts and ability to process information? Be specific. Give an example of something you were thinking and how it changed with Relate to Others.

Spirit – when you Relate to Others, what shift do you experience in your mood, feelings, and emotions? Be specific.

CHAPTER SEVEN

Speak Your Mind

"It does not require many words to speak the truth."
~Chief Joseph

I met Jenny, a small woman with a pipsqueak voice, at one of my yoga teacher trainings. During the training, our teacher often criticized her for talking too softly and not commanding her classes. He accused her of never speaking her mind. As a result, when she would practice teach we either couldn't hear her, or didn't trust her ability to lead. When asked to speak up, she tried shouting and her voice got squeaky and harsh. Our teacher coached her to stand tall, breathe deep, align her head and neck and connect with her belly and core before teaching. By the end of the weeklong retreat, when she got up to practice teach the 65 students in the class, we could hear her, even in the back row. Her pipsqueak voice had a deep resonance to it that we could hear and feel her even when she whispered.

A few weeks after the training ended, she emailed all of her classmates a story about her ability to speak her mind. Her husband asked her to lead a yoga class for 200 U.S. Marines. When she arrived, she discovered the facility couldn't provide her with a microphone. Before she began teaching, remembering what our teacher had taught her, she stood up tall like a Marine at attention, took several deep breaths and focused on bringing her voice up from her core. Even the Marines in the back corner of the room could hear her, and at the end of the class she was complimented on her ability to command respect and hold authority over such an intimidating room of men.

Jenny always thought she was a pipsqueak. When our yoga training teacher encouraged her to believe in herself and speak from her power, Jenny found her *muchness* and was able to speak her mind in a voice she didn't know she had inside herself. She applied the MOZI Speak Your Mind technique and was able to teach yoga to a roomful of two hundred Marines without a microphone, and her *muchness* was heard and felt by every last one of them.

Benefits of Speak Your Mind

- Releases tension in the neck and shoulders
- Decreases occurrence of headaches
- Supports balance
- Opens the airway
- Lowers risk of injury, particularly in the neck
- Releases jaw tension
- Reduces intensity of TMJ
- Clears sinus blockage and tension
- Improves breathing
- Decreases occurrence of sore throats and laryngitis
- Improves hearing and listening
- Connects the head to the heart
- Clears the head and provides a sense of calm
- Promotes a resonant quality in the voice
- Creates a deeper and fuller voice
- Improves speaking and listening skills
- Supports honest communication
- Promotes ability to speak from the heart

Speak Your Mind Pre-Test

Answer the following questions based on how you feel RIGHT NOW

I feel pain in my teeth, tongue, mouth, jaw, and/or neck.
Agree   5   4   3   2   1   0   Disagree

I feel expressive and communicative.
Agree   5   4   3   2   1   0   Disagree

I feel capable of handling stress in the areas of communication.
Agree   5   4   3   2   1   0   Disagree

I feel able to process information, both that which comes into me and goes out of me.
Agree   5   4   3   2   1   0   Disagree

I feel able and willing to share what I think and feel.
Agree   5   4   3   2   1   0   Disagree

Journal

Write about times in your life when speaking your mind through better access to your internal true voice and expression would be helpful. Write about times in your life when you felt you didn't say what you meant or get your point across effectively when it was important, were challenged in your ability to share how you felt, or were unable to be clear in what you mean. Write about times your felt like you struggled with a failure to communicate. Include both physical ailments of the neck, mouth, and jaw and metaphorical situations of feeling tight lipped or like a cat got your tongue.

Speak Your Mind Technique

1. Stand tall and put your finger on chin to tuck it in.
2. Push the back of your head back to the wall behind you.
3. Lift the crown of your head up to feel your neck and spine get longer.
4. Keep this alignment of your skull balanced over your neck.
5. Begin focused breathing.
6. Affirm to yourself, "I am clear, expressive, and communicative."
7. Make a few notes here of what differences you notice from before employing the Speak Your Mind technique to after.

Homework

Practice this Speak Your Mind Technique every time you are about to address an individual or a group: answering the phone, giving a presentation or speech, sharing important information with someone, addressing a service worker or clerk, etc. Make a few notes here about how you feel at the end of the day after practicing this Speak Your Mind technique throughout the day.

Speak Your Mind Post-Test

For best results, practice this exercise for a day or longer before taking the post-test. Then, answer the following questions based on how you feel RIGHT NOW.

I feel pain in my teeth, tongue, mouth, jaw, and/or neck.
Agree   5   4   3   2   1   0   Disagree

I feel expressive and communicative.
Agree   5   4   3   2   1   0   Disagree

I feel capable of handling stress in the areas of communication.
Agree   5   4   3   2   1   0   Disagree

I feel able to process information, both that which comes into me and goes out of me.
Agree   5   4   3   2   1   0   Disagree

I feel able and willing to share what I think and feel.
Agree   5   4   3   2   1   0   Disagree

Compare your answers here to the answers you gave in the pre-test. Make notes here as to the differences:

Questions for Review

Body – when you practice Speak Your Mind alignment, what effects do you notice in your body? Be specific and include which body parts you feel affected and what the effect was.

Mind – when you practice "Speak Your Mind" affirmations, what shift do you experience in your thoughts and ability to process information? Be specific. Give an example of something you were thinking and how it changed with Speak Your Mind.

Spirit – when you Speak Your Mind, what shift do you experience in your mood, feelings, and emotions? Be specific.

CHAPTER EIGHT

Muchness is Contagious

"TERILEIGH!!! YOU ARE A GODDESS!!!" Stunned, I dropped the smoothie from my left hand, stood up taller, and turned my head in the direction of the voice. Marcus had stopped his car in the middle of the street and leaned across the passenger seat to reach to me through the window. As I went to greet him, I glanced at the driver in the convertible behind him and was relieved to see her smiling at me as she took the unexpected stop as an opportunity to put the top down on her car. I waved at her with one hand as I grabbed Marcus' hand in the other. He pulled it to his lips and kissed it as he said, "I'll see you in class," and drove off.

A year earlier, I was teaching a class at the yoga studio where Marcus practiced. I had given him a simple assist with the intention of helping him access more of his strength from his core. After class he told me that my little assist made him feel stronger through the whole practice than he had ever felt in his entire life, including his many years on the football field and thousands of hours of yoga practice. You see, in our first interaction, I had given Marcus as tiny taste of his own *muchness*, and upon our reunion he gave me a taste of my own. The happy woman in the car behind us witnessed the whole exchange and was able to, for a tiny moment, feel *muchness* in herself and shine it out in a grin.

I don't know Marcus well at all. Aside from his Facebook posts occasionally popping up on my newsfeed, I only see him every two or three years when I guest instruct at his home studio in Maryland. We have never had conversation last more than a minute. Yet, whenever we meet, we play a happy little game of catch with a ball of *muchness*, and anyone in the vicinity can't help but get caught up in the game as well.

One of the great things about *muchness* is that it is contagious. I've experienced its contagious qualities through Marcus, my cocky baby brother, a nurturing hotel clerk, and a boisterous Great Dane, not to mention countless other examples. When you do find it in yourself, if even for just a moment, you can't help but to share it, and then the people around you are likely to feel it as well.

I challenge you to make finding your *muchness* an active experience. If I were to passively wait for Marcus to toss me the ball of *muchness* or a random Great Dane to give me a nose-kiss of *muchness* on the cheek, I would only be getting tastes of it every few years or in random unexpected moments. Instead of waiting for it to come to you, go inside yourself and grab it, coax it out from under the covers, pull it out from the bottom of the pile of your priorities, and display it in the direct sunlight of your day.

Finding your *muchness* doesn't have to be hard, and the exercises of the MOZI Experience are designed to be simple, practical, and accessible. Whether you plowed through this book in one sitting, or you methodically worked your way through all the exercises chapter by chapter, or you jumped randomly through excerpts, I hope that at the very least, you were able to gain an understanding that *muchness* is inside you and accessing it in small moments is easy. The key to maintaining your *muchness* is to practice, and practice often, because practice makes progress. If you want to aspire to perfection as in the adage "practice makes perfect," you are reaching to an end point. The key here is that progress is growth, and growth is a journey that can always continue. I invite you to mosey through your practice toward growth and progress.

You don't need to do the exercises in this book precisely in the order in which they were prescribed. If all that you do is remember occasionally to take a deep breath and set a mental intention to whatever action you are doing in the moment, you are practicing the MOZI Method. Like anything, the more you practice, the more you remember.

Like the very first paragraph of this book suggests, everything about you is perfect, including how you choose to apply yourself to the MOZI Experience. There is no wrongness about this process or your experience of it. If something in this book doesn't resonate with you, that's fine. If other things get you super excited, that's fine too. I just hope you can find a way to MOZI, and to MOZI often, because the more you MOZI, the more *muchness* the world will see and be.

CHAPTER NINE

Ways to Mozi

"We don't receive wisdom; we must discover it for ourselves after a journey that no one can take for us or spare us." ~Marcel Proust

There are many ways you can MOZI in addition to reading this book. Become a member of MOZI Online and take part in the MOZI e-learning program. Receive MOZI inspirational emails. Follow MOZI on your favorite social networking sites. Attend a MOZI Training. Participate in a MOZI Yoga Program. You can even get certified as a MOZI licensed instructor.

MOZI Virtual School

At www.moziexperience.com we offer a complete online learning experience where members have access to blogs, instructional

videos, webinars, informational research and other e-learning opportunities. Track your progress, interact with peers, and receive
personalized instructor feedback.

MOZI Online

Engage in MOZI discussions on MOZI's various social networking pages. Share how you MOZI on Facebook. Tweet your own
MOZI musings on Twitter. Find examples of famous people who
lead the way to MOZI on Pinterest. Discover inspirational quotes
that support MOZI-ing on Tumblr. Peruse MOZI images on Flickr.

MOZI Trainings

MOZI offers a six-week interactive training program that is ca-
tered to the individual needs of any organization, corporation,
group, or facility. A certified and licensed MOZI instructor will
coach you through the program with weekly meetings that include
interactive lessons and support group discussions as well as enrollment in MOZI Online and personalized feedback from your instructor. Can't find a MOZI training program near you? Contact us
to bring MOZI to your group or organization. We can cater the
program for corporate trainings, team building, educational staff
development, and self-awareness trainings in non-profit organiza-
tions such as homeless shelters, prisons, and more.

MOZI Yoga Method

Have you already established a yoga practice and want to learn
how to apply MOZI to your practice and find more *muchness* in
your yoga and life? MOZI Yoga can show you how to find that
amazing AHA feeling every single time you step on your mat, and
how to make that feeling last long after you step off your mat.

Bring a MOZI Yoga certified instructor to your home studio or gym or even for a group of your yoga friends in your homes.

MOZI Certification and Licensure

Do you love what you have learned in MOZI and want to share it with others? Become a licensed MOZI instructor and/or a certified MOZI Coach. This intensive training provides you with the training, materials, marketing and promotional packages and mentorship to lead the MOZI Training or consult and coach MOZI clients.

MOZI Business Coaching

Do you own a small business that struggles in some areas or is looking to go to the next level? A licensed MOZI Business Coach can apply the MOZI EXPERIENCE to your business goals by helping establish structure, organization (Stand Your Ground), provide tools to increase creativity and vision (go with the flow), identify and capitalize on your strengths (access your strength), improve customer relations (relate to others), and express your vision through sales and marketing (speak your mind).

MOZI Life Coaching

Do you have challenges in your life that just hold you back, or goals you just can't seem to reach? A licensed MOZI Life Coach can apply the MOZI EXPERIENCE to your challenges and goals and create a personalized MOZI practice to establish support and stability (Stand Your Ground), increase flexibility and freedom (Go With the Flow), improve confidence and self-esteem (Access Your Strength), foster healthy relationships (Relate to Others), and communicate clearly (Speak Your Mind).

MOZI Share

Do you know of an organization or group that could benefit from the MOZI Experience? Contact us and we will send a MOZI certified coach to discuss their needs and individually design and MOZI method for their purposes.

ABOUT THE AUTHOR

With a Master's Degree in Teaching, Teri Leigh has been educating, speaking, and presenting since 1991 with emphasis on clear communication, best practices in education, practical skills application, and effective learning strategies. An Experienced Registered Yoga Teacher with Yoga Alliance, she has led yoga teacher trainings and workshops in over sixty venues nationwide. With spiritual training including Reiki mastership and shamanic eldership, Teri Leigh specializes in teaching the integration of the healing properties of the natural elements (earth, water, fire, nature, mineral) in practical and simplistic applications through corporate training, yoga instruction, and self-awareness and body mechanics workshops.

Made in the USA
Lexington, KY
17 March 2018